I0816209

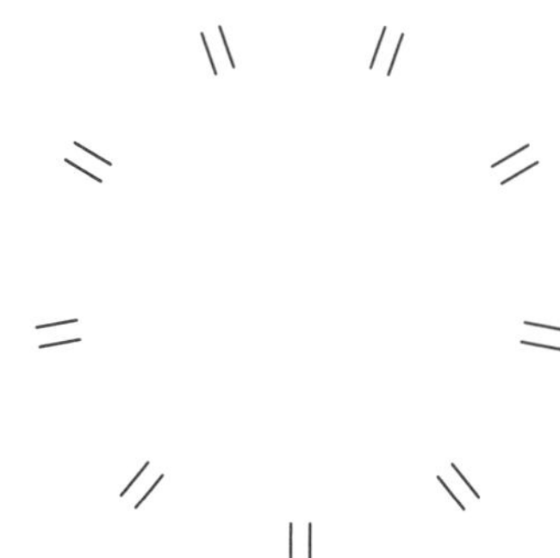

The Service Practice

A Four-Session Guide to Serve in the Way of Jesus

WaterBrook

John Mark Comer and Practicing the Way

WaterBrook
An imprint of the Penguin Random House Christian Publishing Group, a division of Penguin Random House LLC
1745 Broadway, New York, NY 10019
waterbrookmultnomah.com
penguinrandomhouse.com

Scripture quotations are taken from the Holy Bible, New International Version®, NIV®. Copyright © 1973, 1978, 1984, 2011 by Biblica Inc.™ Used by permission of Zondervan. All rights reserved worldwide. (www.zondervan.com). The "NIV" and "New International Version" are trademarks registered in the United States Patent and Trademark Office by Biblica Inc.®

A WaterBrook Trade Paperback Original

Copyright © 2025 by Practicing the Way

Penguin Random House values and supports copyright. Copyright fuels creativity, encourages diverse voices, promotes free speech, and creates a vibrant culture. Thank you for buying an authorized edition of this book and for complying with copyright laws by not reproducing, scanning, or distributing any part of it in any form without permission. You are supporting writers and allowing Penguin Random House to continue to publish books for every reader. Please note that no part of this book may be used or reproduced in any manner for the purpose of training artificial intelligence technologies or systems.

WATERBROOK and colophon are registered trademarks of Penguin Random House LLC.

Published in association with Yates & Yates, www.yates2.com.

All photos courtesy of Practicing the Way.

Trade Paperback ISBN 978-0-593-60339-0
Ebook ISBN 978-0-593-60340-6

Printed in the United States of America on acid-free paper

1st Printing

Book and cover design by Practicing the Way.

For details on special quantity discounts for bulk purchases, contact specialmarketscms@penguinrandomhouse.com.

The authorized representative in the EU for product safety and compliance is Penguin Random House Ireland, Morrison Chambers, 32 Nassau Street, Dublin D02 YH68, Ireland. https://eu-contact.penguin.ie

Contents

PART 01

Getting Started

Welcome

The modern West is consumed with self-interest.

In a culture dominated by consumerism and individualism, the message—not just being told to us, but forming us—is that we must "look out for number one." We are taught, both implicitly and often explicitly, not to "value others above [ourselves],"* as the apostle Paul once wrote, but to do the opposite.

Even when our lives are disrupted by the needs around us, we can feel overwhelmed by the sheer volume of issues we see, paralyzed and uncertain of where to give our attention. Many of us carry a quiet guilt or shame for not doing enough, and yet we still don't know the path forward. In this time of self-focus and overwhelming need, the practice of service, as taught and modeled by Jesus, is vital. Jesus, "the Son of Man [who] did not come to be served, but to serve,"** invites us to follow him in radical service that moves us beyond ourselves and into love.

Service that follows compassion, surrendering plans and expectations.
Service that goes unseen in hidden places.
Service that befriends those we perhaps thought we were above.
Service that, in love, embraces a great cost to ourselves.

In this Practice, we will explore what it looks like to make serving others our way of being in the world—uncovering the why, how, where, and who in Jesus' vision of service. This kind of service will certainly not just happen in our "me-centered," self-gratifying world. It will require practice. But if we say *yes* to Jesus' invitation to attune and attend to the needs around us, it has the potential to do a deep work—not just through us, but in us.

Welcome to the Practice of service.

---

* Philippians 2v3.

** Matthew 20v28.

The Nine Practices

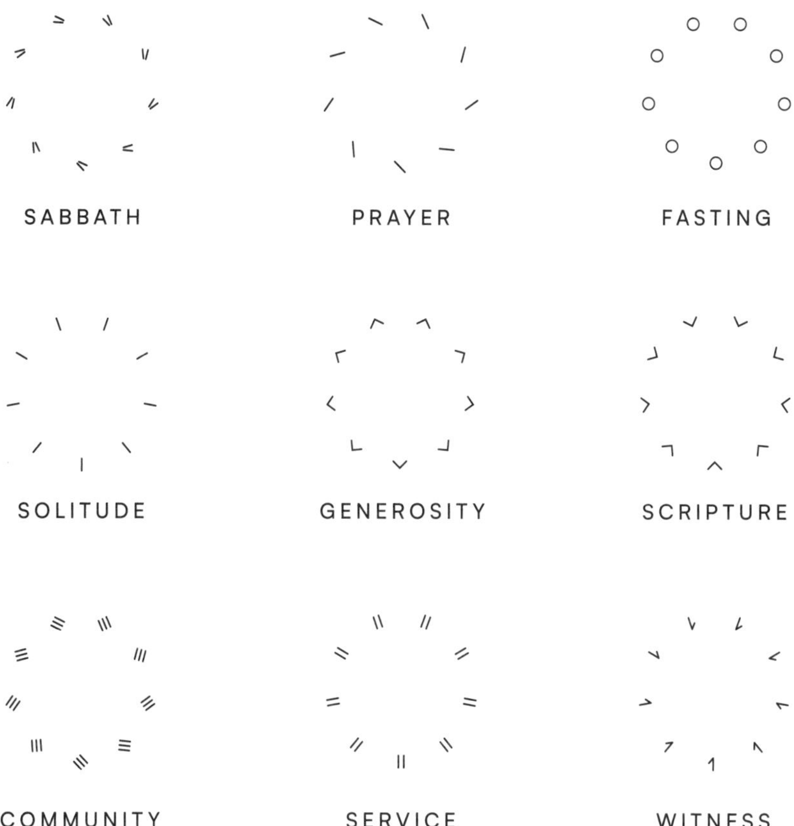

Service is just one of nine core Practices in the body of resources available from Practicing the Way. The Practices are spiritual disciplines centered on the life rhythms of Jesus. They are designed not to add even more to your already overbusy life but to slow you down and create space for the Spirit of God to form you to be with Jesus, become like him, and do what he did. Ultimately, they are a way to experience the love of God.

To run another Practice or learn more, turn to page 106.

How to Use This Guide

A few things you need to know

This Practice is designed to be done in community, whether with a few friends around a table, within your small group, in a larger class format, or with your entire church.

The Practice is four sessions long. We recommend meeting together every week or every other week. For those of you who want to spend more time on this Practice, we've included an additional four weeks of bonus conversations in the appendix to go deeper in Scripture and discussion. You are welcome to pause for these studies in between sessions or skip over them.

You will each need a copy of this Companion Guide. You can purchase a print or ebook version from your preferred retailer or find a free digital PDF version at launch.practicingtheway.org. We recommend the print version so you can stay away from your devices during the Practices, as well as take notes during each session. But we realize that digital works better for some.

Each session should take about one to two hours, depending on how long you allow for discussion and whether or not you begin with a meal. See the sample session on the following page.

Are you a group leader or facilitator? Log in to your online Dashboard or sign up at launch.practicingtheway.org to find ideas, best practices, and tips on running this Practice. Page 110 also offers helpful information and tips.

Our Practices are designed to work in a variety of group sizes and environments. For that reason, your gatherings may include additional elements like meals or worship time, or may follow a structure slightly different from the following sample. Please adapt as you see fit.

Sample Session

Here is what a typical session could look like.

Welcome

Welcome the group and open in prayer.

Introduction (2–3 min.)

Watch the introduction to the session and pause the video when indicated for your first discussion.

Discussion 01: Practice reflection in triads (15–20 min.)

Process your previous week's spiritual exercise in smaller groups of three to five people with the questions in the Guide.

Teaching (20 min.)

Watch the teaching portion of the video.

Discussion 02: Group conversation (15–30 min.)

Pause the video when indicated for a group-wide conversation.

Testimony and tutorial (5–10 min.)

Watch the rest of the video.

Prayer to close

Close by praying the liturgy in the Guide or however you choose.

The Weekly Rhythm

The four sessions of this Practice are designed to follow a four-part rhythm that is based on our model of spiritual formation.

01 Learn

Gather together as a community for an interactive experience of learning about the Way of Jesus through teaching, storytelling, and discussion. Bring your Guide to the session and follow along.

02 Practice

On your own, before the next session, go and "put it into practice," as Jesus himself said.* We will provide weekly spiritual exercises to integrate this practice into your everyday life, as well as recommended resources to go deeper.

03 Reflect

Reflection is key to spiritual formation. After your practice and before the next session, set aside 10–15 minutes to reflect on your experience. Reflection questions are included in this Guide at the end of each session.

04 Process together

When you come back together, watch the introduction, and then start by sharing your reflections with your group. This moment is crucial, because we need one another to process our lives before God and make sense of our stories. If you are meeting in a larger group, you will need to break into smaller subgroups for this conversation so everyone has a chance to share.

---

* Philippians 4v9.

Tips on Beginning a New Practice

This Guide is full of spiritual exercises, time-tested strategies, and good advice on the spiritual discipline of service.

But it's important to note that the Practices are not formulaic. We can't use them to control our spiritual formation, or even our relationship with God. Sometimes they don't even work very well. Over the coming weeks, there may be some days when you feel like a channel of God's love to the world around you, and others when you feel unappreciated and exhausted. That's normal.

The key with the spiritual disciplines is to let go of outcomes and just offer them up to Jesus in love.

Because it's so easy to lose sight of the ultimate aim of a Practice, here are a few tips to keep in mind as you begin practicing service.

01 Start small

Start where you are, not where you "should" be. It's counterintuitive, but the smaller the start, the better chance you have of really sticking to it and growing over time. It's better to integrate service into your life slowly than to commit to an overly ambitious expectation that asks too much of you too soon and risks burning you out a few weeks in.

02 Think subtraction, not addition

The goal here isn't to add service to your already overbusy, overfull life. You are likely already overwhelmed. Instead, think: *How is God inviting me to serve where I already am?*

Formation is about less, not more—about slowing down and simplifying your life around what matters most: life with Jesus.

03 You get out what you put in

The more fully you give yourself to this Practice, the more life-changing it will be; the more you just dabble with it, the more shortcuts you take, the less of an effect it will have on your transformation.

04 Remember the J curve

Experts on learning tell us that mastering a new skill tends to follow a J-shaped curve; we often get worse before we get better.

Service might feel a bit difficult at first; it will get easier over time. Just stay with the Practice.

05 There is no formation without repetition

Spiritual formation is slow, deep, cumulative work that happens over years, not weeks. The goal of this four-week experience is just to get you started on a journey of a lifetime. Upon completion of this Practice, you will have a map for the journey ahead and hopefully some possible companions for the Way.

But what you do next is up to you.

Before You Begin

The following resources are designed to enhance your experience of the Service Practice, but they are entirely optional.

Recommended reading

Reading a book alongside the Practice can greatly enhance your understanding and enjoyment of this discipline. You may love to read, or you may not. For that reason, it's recommended but certainly not required.

The recommended reading for the Service Practice is *The Active Life* by Parker Palmer. Parker is a renowned author, educator, and activist known for his work on leadership, community, and the inner life.

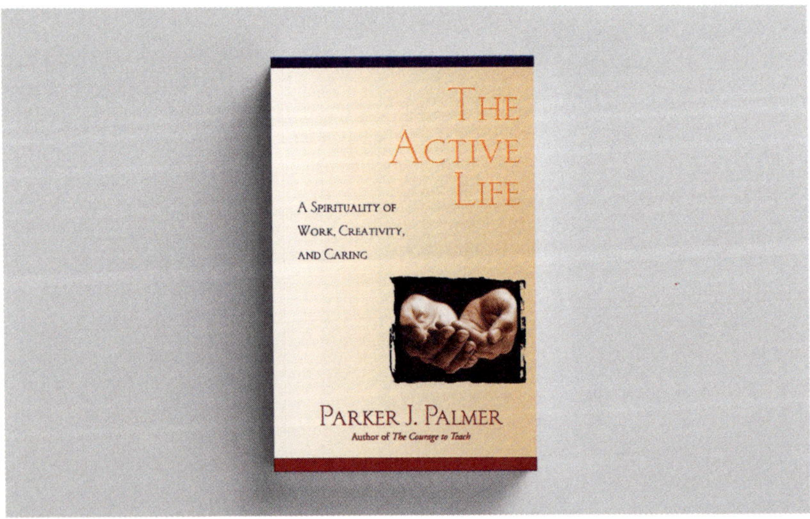

The Spiritual Health Reflection

One final note: Before you begin Session 01, please set aside 20–30 minutes and take the Spiritual Health Reflection. This is a self-assessment we developed in partnership with pastors and leading experts in spiritual formation. It's designed to help you reflect on the health of your soul in order to better name Jesus' invitations to you as you follow the Way.

You can come back to the Spiritual Health Reflection as often as you'd like (we recommend one or two times a year) to chart your growth and continue to move forward on your spiritual journey.

To access the Spiritual Health Reflection, visit practicingtheway.org/reflection and create an account. Answer the prompt questions slowly and prayerfully.

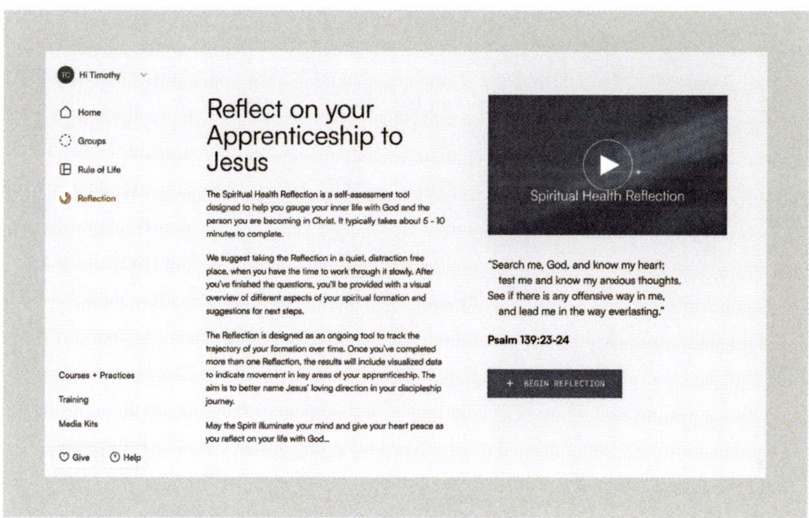

The Practicing the Way Primer

If this is your first time engaging with a Practicing the Way resource, we invite you to set aside 15 minutes before Session 01 to watch a primer on spiritual formation. This will give you a brief overview of the *why* behind spiritual practices and key insights to guard and guide your coming practice.

Log in to your online Dashboard, or sign up to watch the primer at launch.practicingtheway.org.

PART 02

The Sessions

SESSION 01

Love

Overview

Service has always been a defining characteristic of those who apprentice under Jesus.

In the first century, this obscure group, who called themselves "followers of the Way," took their Rabbi Jesus' teachings and example seriously. They called the marginalized "brother" and "sister," cared for the sick at the cost of their own health and reputations, and willingly lived with less so that the needs of others could be met.

In a time when humble service was seen not as a virtue but rather as a duty of the powerless, ordinary people following Jesus chose a wholly different way of relating to those around them.

This kind of life is the result of true spiritual formation—that we would be transformed into people of self-giving love. Maturity, according to Jesus, is *primarily* measured not by our current emotional states, the consistency of our spiritual practices, or even the quality of our moral decisions, but by lives given in loving service to the world around us.

This makes service not just a practice for those of us in Jesus' kingdom, but a gauge of how much his kingdom is truly *in us.*

Opening Questions

When instructed, circle up in triads (smaller groups of three to five people) and discuss the following questions:

01 What brought you to the Service Practice? What are you hoping to see God do in your life through it?

02 What is one question you would like to explore in this Practice?

03 What's your primary feeling around living more deeply in Jesus' vision of service? Excitement? Overwhelm? Inadequacy?

04 Share about a time when someone loved you by meeting one of your practical needs, whether big or small. What made that experience memorable for you?

Teaching

Key Scripture

Matthew 7v16–20

Session summary

- All spiritual practices are meant to transform us into people of love.
- When we mistake the how (spiritual practices) for the why (becoming people of love) in our spiritual formation, we do not bear fruit.
- Our maturity (or fruit) as apprentices of Jesus is evidenced by love practically expressed through service.
- To become a person of love is to be a firstfruits of God's kingdom on earth.
- We step toward this by serving where we are, starting today.

Teaching Notes

As you watch Session 01 together, feel free to use these pages to take notes.

Discussion Questions

Now it's time for a conversation about the teaching. Pause the video for a few minutes to discuss these questions in small groups:

01 What stood out to you from today's teaching? What feelings came up for you throughout it?

02 Consider the implications of Jesus' words about himself: "The Son of Man did not come to be served, but to serve." In what ways do these words inspire or challenge you?

03 How have you typically measured your spiritual "temperature" or health? How is this the same as or different from Jesus' metric of "love expressed through service"?

04 Reflect on where you are currently when it comes to practicing service. What could it look like for you to "start where you are"?

Practice Notes

As you continue to watch Session 01 together, feel free to use this page to take notes.

Closing Prayer

Take a few deep breaths, become aware of God's presence, and pray this prayer slowly, leaving a short silence between each line.

Jesus Christ, you came not to be served,
but to serve. More than giving what you had,
you gave of yourself in love.
Help us to follow you in the way of love—
to be led to people and places we would not
otherwise go if not for you.

Amen.

Exercise

Do one act of service.

For this exercise, start by serving someone in your family or relational circle, not a stranger. This act could be as small as:

- Cleaning the dishes when you don't need to.
- Getting a cup of coffee for a co-worker.
- Running an errand for a neighbor.

You don't need to announce or draw attention to what you're doing—it's okay if it goes unnoticed. Just quietly love this person by meeting a practical need of theirs. And as you serve, let the love of God come through your heart, allowing him to love others through you.

Reach Exercise

Begin serving in the context of your local church.

Find out where there is a need in your community, and make yourself available to meet that need. Consider looking for opportunities that are far from the stage: working in children's ministry, setting up early, caring for the facility, greeting or serving in hospitality, or cleaning up after the gathering.

Practice Reflection

Reflection is a key component in our spiritual formation.

Millennia ago, King David prayed in Psalm 139v23–24:

> Search me, God, and know my heart;
> test me and know my anxious thoughts.
> See if there is any offensive way in me,
> and lead me in the way everlasting.

South African professor Trevor Hudson has quoted one of his pastoral supervisors as saying, "We do not learn from experience; we learn from reflection upon experience."*

If you want to get the most out of this Practice, you need to do it and then reflect on it.

---

* Trevor Hudson, *A Mile in My Shoes: Cultivating Compassion* (Upper Room Books, 2005), 57.

Before your next time together with the group for Session 02, take 10–15 minutes to journal your answers to the following three questions:

01 Where did I feel resistance?

02 Where did I feel joy?

03 Where did I most experience God's nearness?

Note: As you write, be as specific as possible. While bullet points are just fine, if you write out your insights in narrative form, your brain will be able to process them in a more lasting way.

Reflection Notes

ON YOUR OWN — **REFLECT**

Keep Growing (Optional)

The following resources were created to enhance your experience of this Practice, but they are entirely optional.

Read

The Active Life by Parker Palmer (Chapters 01–02)

Listen

Rule of Life podcast on service (Episode 01)

Bonus Conversation

If you would like to slow down this four-week Practice to give your community more time to sit in each week's teaching and spiritual exercise, you can pause and meet for an optional conversation outlined in the appendix.

SESSION 02

Hiddenness

Overview

Where does your imagination go when you consider where you can serve? Perhaps it leads you to your local church, the care home nearby, or the low-income neighborhood in your city.

For some of us, these very well could be the places Jesus is leading us to give more of ourselves—more on that in the sessions to come. But if we consider Jesus' life, and specifically the environments where he chose to serve, we see a recurring theme: Jesus often served in very ordinary spaces—in homes and marketplaces, at water wells and dinner tables, even in what we could call his "daily commute."

What if our greatest opportunities to practice loving service are not in places we have yet to enter, but where we already are? Familiar places like our offices, homes, and neighborhoods—among people who know us and whom we know in return.

For most of us, serving in these environments is much more challenging than picking up a ladle at a soup kitchen or mowing a stranger's lawn. But when we choose to serve in them anyway, these environments become places of deep formation where we can be transformed into people of love.

Reflection Questions

When instructed, circle up in triads (smaller groups of three to five people) and discuss the following questions:

01 Share about this week's exercise of one act of service: What did you do, and what was your experience like?

02 What reflections do you have on God's love being expressed through ordinary acts like these?

03 What internal motivations do you notice typically driving you to acts like these?

04 How did the person you served respond, if at all, and how did their response, or lack of response, impact you?

Teaching

Key Scripture

John 13v15

Session summary

- Service is meant to be practiced in our current and close environments, not just in new and distant ones.
- Jesus modeled this ordinary form of service by washing his closest followers' feet.
- Service—perhaps more than other spiritual practices—can be pursued with the wrong motive: to be seen or to feel good.
- To avoid this, we can choose for some of our service to be done in hiddenness.
- When done in secret, service shapes not just what we do, but what God does in us.

Teaching Notes

As you watch Session 02 together, feel free to use these pages to take notes.

Discussion Questions

Now it's time for a conversation about the teaching. Pause the video for a few minutes to discuss these questions in small groups:

01 What invitations or confrontations did you experience through today's teaching?

02 What ordinary, everyday people or places came to your mind as opportunities for service?

03 Why do you think we often associate service with more distant contexts rather than with our closest relationships and immediate surroundings? Do you see this tendency in your own life, and why might that be?

04 In what ways have you personally experienced the tension of serving for recognition versus serving out of genuine love?

Practice Notes

As you continue to watch Session 02 together, feel free to use this page to take notes.

Closing Prayer

End your time together by praying this liturgy:

Help us, Father, to remember that your
loving gaze is always upon us,
that no good deed escapes your
delighted attention. Lead us to serve
in familiar and hidden places, beyond
all other rewarding eyes but yours.

Amen.

Exercise

This week, we invite you to do one hidden act of service.

It's the same as last week: to find a person in your ordinary life to serve in just one small way. But this time, try and keep it hidden—or at least really, really quiet. This might look like:

- Anonymously buying flowers for someone.
- Dropping off a meal for someone in need and not telling anyone about it.
- Volunteering for a local charity but not telling any of your friends.

As you serve, pay attention to your heart's desire to be seen. Talk to God about it. Let God free your heart from the approval or disapproval of others.

Reach Exercise

For this week's reach exercise, we have a guided listening prayer.

The idea of this exercise is to set aside time to listen to God for where he is leading you to serve.

There are far more needs in the world than any of us could possibly meet. To avoid things like burnout and compassion fatigue, it's very important that we learn to discern where God is leading us to serve to play our small part in his kingdom.

There are five simple steps to this exercise:

01 Pick an ordinary environment you're already part of—your home, your neighborhood, your workplace, your church community. The goal is not to find a new cause or place to serve, but to pay attention to where your life already intersects with others.

Circle the environment you want to focus on in your time of prayer:

My home **My workplace**

My neighborhood **My church community**

02 Ask the Holy Spirit to speak to you—inviting you to discern whom he may be drawing your attention to and how you might serve them in that space.

03 Wait. Sit quietly for a few minutes before God with an open heart and a listening posture. Set a timer for yourself if that is helpful.

04 Write down anything that comes to mind—whether it's a person, a need, a specific way to serve, or even just a nudge to be more present somewhere.

05 Finally, act on one of those ideas this coming week. Don't wait too long—just respond to the Spirit's promptings.

If possible, write below when and how you plan to act on what the Spirit has led you toward.

Practice Reflection

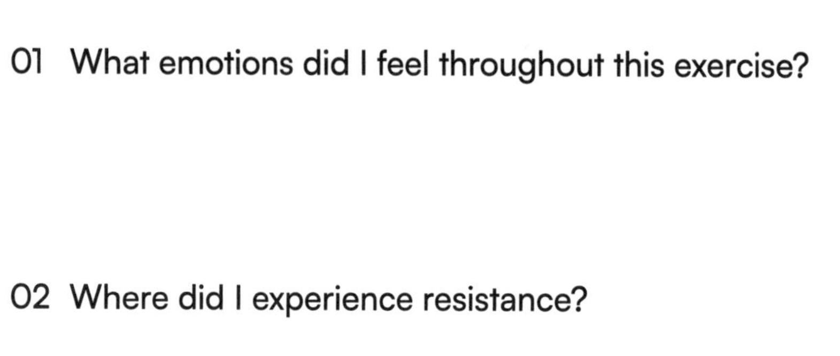

Before your next time together with the group for Session 03, take 10–15 minutes to journal your answers to the following three questions:

01 What emotions did I feel throughout this exercise?

02 Where did I experience resistance?

03 What invitation(s) from God do I sense here?

Note: As you write, be as specific as possible. While bullet points are just fine, if you write out your insights in narrative form, your brain will be able to process them in a more lasting way.

Reflection Notes

Keep Growing (Optional)

The following resources were created to enhance your experience of this Practice, but they are entirely optional.

Read

The Active Life by Parker Palmer (Chapters 03–04)

Listen

Rule of Life podcast on service (Episode 02)

Bonus Conversation

If you would like to slow down this four-week Practice to give your community more time to sit in each week's teaching and spiritual exercise, you can pause and meet for an optional conversation outlined in the appendix.

SESSION 03

Availability

Overview

Jesus lived a remarkably interruptible life. More than 30 stories in *The Gospel of Mark* alone hinge on Jesus' ability to see an interruption as an invitation. And these are just the stories that were recorded from his life. We can never know just how many people received Jesus' loving attention and service in these unplanned moments.

This way of being in the world is about more than our personalities—whether we consider ourselves more planned or spontaneous. It's about practicing radical availability—about considering that seemingly annoying distractions in life may actually be holy disruptions.

Some of the most beautiful opportunities for service pass us by unknowingly in the ordinary movements of our days, while our attention is fixed on our plans rather than the people God loves right in front of us. The invitation, by God's grace, is for us to become the kinds of people who increasingly see the needs around us and stop to serve them.

That, like the good Samaritan in Jesus' famous parable, we might be those who choose not to walk by on the other side but to cross over in compassion.

Reflection Questions

When instructed, circle up in triads (smaller groups of three to five people) and discuss the following questions:

01 Without sharing what you did for this week's exercise, describe your experience. What emotions came up for you before or during it?

02 In what ways did you experience personal resistance or confrontation during the exercise?

03 What was the same or different for you in your experience of this week's exercise compared to the previous week? Why do you think that is?

04 What invitation do you sense from God for how you are to view hiddenness or incorporate it going forward from this Practice?

Teaching

Key Scripture

Matthew 22v37–39

Session summary

- Jesus taught and modeled living an interruptible life that turned strangers into neighbors.
- Jesus invites us to adopt two postures as we follow him:
    - **Intentionality**—the practice of purposefully ordering our lives around God and his way
    - **Interruptibility**—the capacity to see a need and stop to meet it
- We may find one of these postures more natural than the other, though both are vital in our apprenticeship to Jesus.
- The kingdom comes when we serve others like Jesus—in both big and small ways, in both intentional and spontaneous acts done with great love.
- If shame is a disconnector between us and God, and us and one another, confession is the great reconnector.

Teaching Notes

As you watch Session 03 together, feel free to use these pages to take notes.

Discussion Questions

Now it's time for a conversation about the teaching. Pause the video for a few minutes to discuss these questions in small groups:

01 Which people or issues do you notice cause you to experience "from-the-gut compassion"?

02 On a scale of 1 to 10, with 1 being not interruptible and 10 being very interruptible, where would you place yourself today? What reflections do you have on the number you gave?

03 What might be some reasons you find yourself "passing by on the other side" of certain needs around you?

04 The invitation here is not to try to meet every need around us. With that in mind, what need(s) do you feel compelled to begin "crossing to the other side" to meet?

Practice Notes

As you continue to watch Session 03 together, feel free to use this page to take notes.

Closing Prayer

End your time together by praying this liturgy:

Jesus Christ, come to us
in holy surprise and interruption.
Come to us in the least and
the looked over.
Give us your eyes to see,
your compassion to stop,
and your courage to serve.

Amen.

Exercise

Do one unplanned act of service.

This week, we invite you to do one unplanned act of service—to embrace an interruption and respond with service instead of impatience or annoyance.

You might consider beginning each day by inviting the Spirit's holy interruptions into your day. Or pray the Examen each evening, reviewing the day with God and asking the Spirit to highlight the holy interruptions you engaged or missed.

This at least means going a bit slower through your week and keeping your eyes open for interruptions that may be God-initiated. And if no noticeable interruption comes, then just go wherever you see a need, and meet that need.

Reach Exercise

Do an audit of your schedule, and cut at least one thing out.

For most of us, becoming more interruptible begins with creating more room to be interrupted in the first place.

Look over your weekly schedule, make a list of all your commitments, and ask yourself whether you have enough margin in your life to be available for both intentionality and interruptibility. If the answer is *no* (and it's highly likely it will be), then find at least one thing to step away from to create space for responding to holy interruptions.

01 Take a moment to write down all your commitments in a given week. This should include things like household responsibilities, social engagements, leisure activities, and daily habits.

02 Looking at your commitments, ask yourself: *Do I have enough time and space to be intentionally present and interruptible for needs that come up?*

03 Choose at least one commitment or activity that you intend to remove this week, and cross it out on the previous page. This may be something you intend to remove from your weekly rhythm going forward or just for this week as an offering of space to God.

04 Take some time to reflect. When and how will you make this change? How much time does removing this commitment give back to you? How do you feel about making this adjustment?

05 Finish your time in prayer. Invite God to fill this time with opportunities to love and serve people in both planned and spontaneous ways.

Practice Reflection

Before your next time together with the group for Session 04, take 10–15 minutes to journal your answers to the following three questions:

01 What emotions did I experience when paying attention to the needs around me?

02 What resistance to being interrupted did I encounter this week?

03 What might God be speaking to me through these interruptions?

Note: As you write, be as specific as possible. While bullet points are just fine, if you write out your insights in narrative form, your brain will be able to process them in a more lasting way.

Reflection Notes

ON YOUR OWN — REFLECT

Keep Growing (Optional)

The following resources were created to enhance your experience of this Practice, but they are entirely optional.

Read

The Active Life by Parker Palmer (Chapters 05–06)

Listen

Rule of Life podcast on service (Episode 03)

Bonus Conversation

If you would like to slow down this four-week Practice to give your community more time to sit in each week's teaching and spiritual exercise, you can pause and meet for an optional conversation outlined in the appendix.

ABSINTHE
DUCROS fils
TRIPLE RECTIFICATION

SESSION 04

Kinship

Overview

We would have to ignore large portions of Scripture to avoid God's concern for the poor and his desire for his people to care for them. In the first century, the poor or "the needy" would have included widows, orphans, or those in prison.

Today, this could be children in the foster care system, single parents, the sick, the elderly on fixed incomes, and refugees.

While our societal order often overlooks these individuals and keeps them on the margins, Jesus' order—or the kingdom of heaven—moves them toward equal ground at the center. Jesus so identifies with and cares for the poor that following him means we must also brush shoulders with the needy. And more than that, we must see *in each of them* a brother and a sister.

This is what distinguishes service in the way of Jesus: We are invited beyond charity from afar into love up close—to leave ourselves open to the reality that service may turn strangers not only into neighbors but also into family.

This is the dignifying destination that true service leads us toward: kinship.

Reflection Questions

When instructed, circle up in triads (smaller groups of three to five people) and discuss the following questions:

01 What did you end up doing for this week's exercise of an unplanned act of service?

02 How did you notice this exercise impact the way you went about your week and what you were paying attention to?

03 What resistance did you experience to being interrupted?

04 How has this exercise impacted the way you see interruptions?

Teaching

Key Scripture

Luke 16v19–31

Session summary

- Jesus orders his kingdom opposite to the world's social order—placing the marginalized at the center.
- To be in fellowship with Jesus means to be in fellowship with the marginalized.
- Jesus' vision for service is rooted in kinship, not simply acting as a service provider.
- Kinship means embracing people who are not biologically family as brothers and sisters.
- We serve in pursuit of kinship—not because it works, but because every individual is worth it.

Teaching Notes

As you watch Session 04 together, feel free to use these pages to take notes.

Discussion Questions

Now it's time for a conversation about the teaching. Pause the video for a few minutes to discuss these questions in small groups:

01 What stood out to you from the teaching on the parable of the rich man and Lazarus?

02 How does Jesus' vision for service, not as distant charity but as kinship, inspire or confront you?

03 In what ways have you noticed yourself avoiding the kinds of environments or people that Jesus sought out? What might be holding you back from developing relationships in those contexts?

04 In what ways can you develop a deeper, more relational approach to serving those who are typically seen as "other" in your life?

Practice Notes

As you continue to watch Session 04 together, feel free to use this page to take notes.

Closing Prayer

End your time together by praying this liturgy:

Father, help us remember that
despite our own poverty of spirit,
you have made the kingdom ours
and welcomed us into family.
Let us set our tables widely, that
you may bring to us strangers whom
we someday call brothers and sisters.

Amen.

Exercise

Do one act of service for someone in need.

In *The Book of Acts*, a synonym for *the poor* is the phrase "those who had need" or "the needy." In the first century, this would have been widows, orphans, and those in prison.

In our time, this could be kids in the foster care system, the elderly living on fixed incomes, single parents, the sick, those dying in hospice, those in prison, and refugees. The reality is that all around, often hiding in plain sight, are people who are in need. This week, go serve them.

You can do this through one of two avenues:

01 Volunteer at a local nonprofit.

02 Go directly to someone you have a relational connection to.

Keep in mind that kinship is often cultivated slowly through regularly serving the same need among common people—so consider making a commitment to weekly, biweekly, or monthly service as you're able.

Reach Exercise

Take time to listen and learn a person's story.

As you are serving those in need, find a person you feel a leading to, and go listen and learn. Ask them questions about their story. Listen attentively.

One of the most powerful ways we can love others is by listening deeply to their stories. The purpose of this exercise is to open your heart to kinship—to see them not as an object of your pity, but as a brother or sister.

Practice Reflection

As you come to the end of this Practice, take 10–15 minutes to journal your answers to the following three questions.

01 What fears or hesitations did I experience?

02 What emotions or thoughts was I surprised by?

03 How did I encounter Jesus through the poor?

Note: As you write, be as specific as possible. While bullet points are just fine, if you write your insights out in narrative form, your brain will be able to process them in a more lasting way.

Reflection Notes

ON YOUR OWN — **REFLECT**

Keep Growing (Optional)

The following resources were created to enhance your experience of this Practice, but they are entirely optional.

Read

The Active Life by Parker Palmer (Chapters 07–08)

Listen

Rule of Life podcast on service (Episode 04)

Bonus Conversation

If you would like to slow down this four-week Practice to give your community more time to sit in each week's teaching and spiritual exercise, you can pause and meet for an optional conversation outlined in the appendix.

Christ has no body but yours,

No hands, no feet on earth but yours,

Yours are the eyes through which he looks
with compassion on this world,

Yours are the feet with which he
walks to do good,

Yours are the hands with which he
blesses all the world.

So may you, like Christ, go now not to
be served but to serve.

PART 03

Continue the Journey

Recommended Reading

Here are some of our favorite books on the practice of service for those of you who desire to learn more:

Cruciformity

by Michael J. Gorman

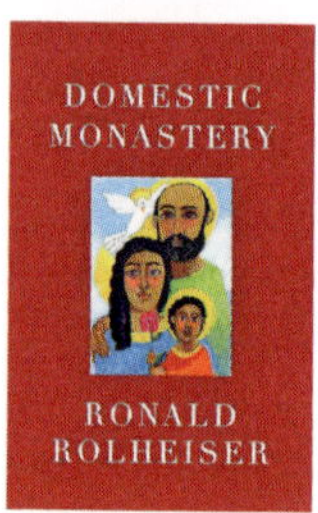

Domestic Monastery

by Ronald Rolheiser

The Deeply Formed Life

by Rich Villodas

Specifically Chapter 09 on "Missional Presence in a Distracted and Disengaged World"

The Holy Longing

by Ronald Rolheiser

Specifically Chapter 08 on "A Spirituality of Justice and Peacemaking"

Invitation to a Journey

by M. Robert Mullholland, Jr.

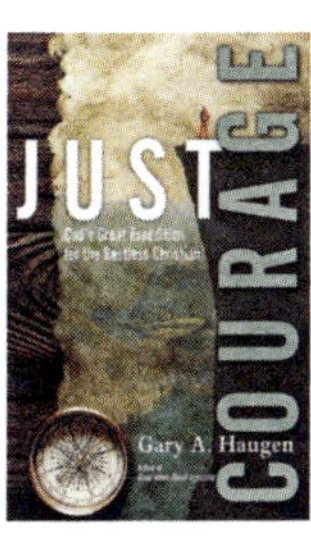

Just Courage

by Gary A. Haugen

Rich Christians in an Age of Hunger

by Ronald J. Sider

The Practices

Information alone isn't enough to produce transformation.

By adopting not just the teaching but the practices from Jesus' own life, we open up our entire beings to God and allow him to transform us into people of love.

Our nine core Practices work together to form a Rule of Life for the modern era.

Sabbath	**Prayer**	**Fasting**
Solitude	**Generosity**	**Scripture**
Community	**Service**	**Witness**

WHAT'S INCLUDED IN EACH PRACTICE

Four Sessions

Each session includes teaching, guided discussion, and weekly exercises to integrate the Practices into daily life.

Companion Guide

A detailed guide provides question prompts, session-by-session exercises, and space to write and reflect.

Recommended Resources

Additional recommended readings and podcasts offer a way to get the most out of the Practices.

Learn more by visiting practicingtheway.org/resources.

The Practicing the Way Course

An eight-session primer on spiritual formation

Two thousand years ago, Jesus said to his disciples, "Follow me." But what does it mean for us to follow Jesus today?

The Practicing the Way Course is an on-ramp to spiritual formation, exploring what it means to follow Jesus and laying the foundation for a life of apprenticeship to him.

WHAT'S INCLUDED

Eight Sessions

John Mark and other voices teaching on apprenticing under Jesus, spiritual formation, healing from sin, meeting God in pain, crafting a Rule of Life, living in community, and more

Exercises

Weekly practices and exercises to help integrate what you've learned into your everyday life

Guided Conversations

Prompts to reflect on your experience and process honestly in community

Companion Guide

A detailed workbook with exercises, space to write and reflect, and suggestions for supplemental resources

Learn more by visiting practicingtheway.org/resources.

Practicing the Way: *Be with him. Become like him. Do as he did.*

The first followers of Jesus developed a Rule of Life, or habits and practices based on the life of Jesus himself. As they learned to live like their teacher, they became people who made space for God to do his most transformative work in their lives.

Practicing the Way is a vision for the future, shaped by the wisdom of the past. It's an introduction to spiritual formation accessible to both beginners and lifelong followers of Jesus, and a companion to the Practicing the Way Course. This book offers theological substance, astute cultural insight, and practical wisdom for creating a Rule of Life in the modern age.

You can order your copy or get copies for your community at practicingtheway.org/book or through your preferred bookseller.

The Circle

Practicing the Way is a nonprofit that develops spiritual formation resources for churches and small groups learning how to become apprentices in the Way of Jesus.

We believe one of the greatest needs of our time is for people to discover how to become lifelong disciples of Jesus. To that end, we help people learn how to be with Jesus, become like him, and do as he did, through the practices and rhythms he and his earliest followers lived by.

All of our downloadable ministry resources are available at no cost, thanks to the generosity of The Circle and other givers from around the world who partner with us to see formation integrated into the church at large.

To learn more or join us, visit practicingtheway.org/give.

For Facilitators

Before you begin, there are three easy things you need to do. (This should take only 10–15 minutes.)

01 Go to launch.practicingtheway.org, log in, create a group, and send a digital invitation to your community. This will give your group access to the Spiritual Health Reflection, videos, and all sorts of valuable extras. Encourage your group to bring along their Companion Guides to each session, as they contain the discussion questions and space to take notes.

- You can purchase a print or ebook version from your preferred retailer or find a free digital PDF version at launch.practicingtheway.org. We recommend the print version so you can stay away from your devices during the Practices, as well as take notes during each session. But we realize that digital works better for some.
- Note: You can order the Guides ahead of time and have them waiting when people arrive for Session 01, or encourage people to order or download their own and bring them to your gatherings.

02 Send a message to your group encouraging everyone to take the Spiritual Health Reflection before your first gathering, which can be found at launch.practicingtheway.org.

03 If your group has not been through the Practicing the Way Course, invite them to watch this short primer before you gather for Session 01 of this Practice.

For training, tips, and more resources for facilitating the Service Practice, log in to the Dashboard at launch.practicingtheway.org.

APPENDIX

Bonus Conversations

For those of you who want to spend longer sitting in this Practice, we've included an additional four weeks of material in this Guide to go deeper in Scripture and discussion.

You are welcome to pause in between sessions for these additional conversations or skip over them.

Love

Many words have been written and spoken about Jesus' washing his disciples' feet. Such an act from someone of Jesus' status was not just uncommon but entirely unheard of. No wonder his disciple Peter interrupts him. Not only was this an act of remarkably humble service, but it was also done for those who, in many cases, are the hardest to serve in that way—those closest to us. And in that very place, with dusty knees and wet hands, he speaks this new command to his disciples: "Go and do the same."

Read John 13v34

Discuss the Scripture

01 Consider what Jesus meant by this being a *new* command. How is his love different from other forms of love?

02 Take a few moments to mentally note or even write down the different ways Jesus loved people in the Gospels. Which examples of his love most challenge or confront you?

03 If you were to survey your life, what are your guiding criteria for whom you consider "worthy" of your love and service?

04 What is one practical step you could take this week to demonstrate love and humility in the way Jesus did?

Discuss the practice

01 What did you decide to do for your one act of service this week?

02 How do you commonly show love to those around you? Is this type of practical service more unnatural or natural for you?

03 How does serving someone you know well differ for you from serving someone new or unfamiliar? Which is more difficult for you?

04 What other inner or outer barriers make it difficult for you to serve others in genuine love? How might you address these barriers in the coming week?

Repeat the exercise

For this week, we invite you to repeat the exercise on page 30 or to try the reach exercise if you have not already.

Hiddenness

The Pharisees were known not only for how they strictly followed each letter of the law but also for taking the opportunity to practice that law in front of others. The problem with this was not that they were *seen* doing good, but that they were doing good *to be seen.* In one of Jesus' most famous teachings—the Sermon on the Mount—he confronts this way of doing good head-on. His counteroffer? We must start keeping secrets—the good kind—between us and our heavenly Father, especially if we hope to discover the rewards that only he can give.

Read Matthew 6v2–4

Discuss the Scripture

01 How do you notice our surrounding culture doing good "to be honored by others"?

02 What do you find most often motivates you to serve others in life? How does this teaching from Jesus align with or confront those motives?

03 What is most challenging for you personally about the prospect of doing good in secret?

04 Though it is a great mystery, what have you experienced to be the Father's rewards for the good you have done in secret?

Discuss the practice

01 On a scale of 1 to 10, how important is recognition to you when doing good for other people? What are your reflections on your number?

02 How do you think people can fend off the apathy and bitterness that sometimes follow good deeds that go unrecognized?

03 How did this act of hidden service influence your view or experience of God's approval versus human approval?

04 If you were to continue serving others often in unseen ways, what kind of person would that form you into?

Repeat the exercise

For this week, we invite you to repeat the exercise on page 50 or to try the reach exercise if you have not already.

Availability

Jesus walked the earth with a kind of availability that we rarely witness in our busy, preoccupied times. Over and over again, throughout the Gospels, he dignifies the needy instead of dismissing them, showing them to be worthy of loving attention. Unlike the crowd, for Jesus, voices like those of the two blind men were loud but not easily ignored. The question for all of us from a story like today's is this: Will we treat those in need along our paths with indifference like the crowd, or with compassion like Jesus?

Read Matthew 20v29–34

Discuss the Scripture

01 What stands out to you from this story?

02 Whom do you most identify with in this story—the blind men, the crowd, or Jesus—and why?

03 What do you think deforms compassion for others in our world today? How can we guard against this?

04 What needs around you seem to be shouting "all the louder" in your heart and mind since starting this Practice?

Discuss the practice

01 What kinds of expectations and hopes did you have going into this week's unplanned act of service?

02 Would you consider yourself more planned or spontaneous? How did that influence your engagement with the exercise?

03 In what ways did this exercise increase your awareness of God's activity in everyday moments?

04 What steps might you take to cultivate a more open posture toward interruptions beyond this exercise?

Repeat the exercise

For this week, we invite you to repeat the exercise on page 72 or to try the reach exercise if you have not already.

Kinship

Jesus both taught and lived by an order upside down from that of the world. In his day, to eat with someone meant you identified with them. Jesus flips not just the cultural expectations but our human defaults on their heads by encouraging his hearers to identify with the needy, not just the noble. And when we compare this passage to many others like it in Scripture, we come to see that Jesus is not ultimately saying, "Do not invite your brothers and sisters," but rather, "These, *too*, are your brothers and sisters." This way of seeing the often-overlooked, according to Jesus, means you are right on the brink of blessedness.

Read Luke 14v12–14

Discuss the Scripture

01 Do you notice yourself offering preferential treatment to those of a "higher" social status? How so?

02 What reflections do you have on serving in ways that cannot be repaid? What about this inspires or confronts you?

03 Take a mental survey of those who typically sit with you around your dinner table. How does this teaching from Jesus speak to that?

04 What could it look like to take one step closer to the vision Jesus is laying out for us in this passage?

Discuss the practice

01 What did you decide to do for your one act of service to someone in need?

02 Did this act of serving challenge any of your preconceived notions about people in need? How so?

03 What internal shifts—such as feelings of empathy, discomfort, or gratitude—did you notice during or after this exercise? What prompted those feelings?

04 What reflections do you have on moving beyond service provider to kinship after this week's act of service?

Repeat the exercise

For this week, we invite you to repeat the exercise on page 94 or to try the reach exercise if you have not already.

To inquire about ordering this Companion Guide in bulk quantities for your church, small group, or staff, contact churches@penguinrandomhouse.com.